An Unlikely Journey

Surviving, Celebrating, and Coping with Your Life

by Scott J. Watson

with Stephanie Hill

Scott J. Watson

First Printing, 2015

ISBN 978-1-50611-963-2

This book is designed to offer suggestions for your journey. Hopefully it will be both fun and
useful. Nothing in this book is designed to be clinical in nature or to take the place of professional
assessment, therapy, or medical intervention.

For questions regarding the use and permissions of this book, contact Scott J. Watson at
scottwatson@heartlandintervention.com.

Contents

Introduction
"It's a Beautiful Day to Be Alive."

One of the reasons I love my neighbor Bill is that he seems to own every tool ever made. That's cool! But what is cooler is that he knows how to use them. Some folks are good with mechanics, and some are not. I can hammer with a screwdriver. I can just turn it around and beat the heck out of something. Even though a screwdriver can be used like a hammer, if I go to the toolbox and get a hammer, there is no way I can make it work like a wrench.

My frustration level would be really high if I were to just wander into Bill's garage and try and figure out how to use all of those tools. There are so many and I'm just not wired to be one of those "Mr. Fix it" types. In life there are a lot of tools, too, tools that folks can use when challenges get in their way. That's what this book is about. My goal is to tell some stories that offer real suggestions, or tools, designed to help you be comfortable in your own skin. I didn't used to know how to use many of these tools either. In fact, these tools used to irritate me. But here's the truth: When I'm having a good day, I don't really need the tools. However, when my hair is burning and my butt is falling off or when things really are not going my way, I *need* the tools. They help me maintain my composure, not damage my relationships, and recover my peace of mind. These tools are individualized; what works for me might not work for you. The tools that have saved you may not be tools I'm ready to try yet.

My life has been impacted by a number of tools that came disguised as suggestions and cutesy, little slogans. For instance: Donny is a guy I know and like. Each time we are together he's likely to say, "I don't know if you've noticed, but it's a beautiful day to be alive." One early morning I was driving from Indianapolis to Nashville, and it was jet-black dark outside. At 4:30 a.m. I was exhausted and grumpy that work had me up so early. However, about forty-five minutes south of Indianapolis, the sky outside my left window started to change colors as the sun came up. I'm getting old; it's not like that was first time I'd ever seen the sun rise. But how many beautiful days had I missed

5

because I was just going about my business and failed to notice? How many beautiful days have *you* missed? That morning as I drove, looking out my window, I could hear Donny's voice in my head. Outside there were corn fields, and the sky was changing; and suddenly, I wasn't thinking, *Oh man, I have a five hour drive to Nashville. It's six in the morning. I'm tired.* No, instead I was thinking, *It's a beautiful day to be alive!*

Slogans helped change my life. Oddly enough, I used to react to them with anger and frustration. "Let go and let God." "Easy does it." "Fake it until you make it." "One day at a time." "Keep it simple, sweetheart." "Keep coming back; it works if you work it." "Life's a garden; dig it." "Keep digging; there's a pony in here somewhere." "If you always do what you always did, you always get what you always got." "Will the defendant please rise?" These simple slogans or phrases often pop into my head—even the ones that used to frustrate me. Now, this collection of slogans has become one of the many tools I can use when times are tough. In addition to slogans, I use readings, journaling, prayer, meditation, and of course, people. These function just like the tools lying around in my neighbor's garage. They are available and can be useful, if I only ask for help and learn how to use them. Some of us need hammers, and some of us need screwdrivers. Some of us are encouraged by slogans and others by books, and most of us are encouraged by many of the tools in our emotional toolboxes. The key is to get the tools out. The key is to learn to use them. Hammers are great, but if you never take them out of the toolbox, the nail won't move.

The bad news is that I'm not an author. The worse news is that I'm a therapist. Since 2007, I have been working to help those struggling in a variety of areas. Much of my experience didn't grow out of education or textbooks, though I have done that work. My diplomas and certificates are in my file cabinet gathering dust. Instead, my experience comes from the lessons that I've learned— both personally, from my own struggles, and professionally, from helping others as a Licensed Clinical Addictions Counselor and Substance Abuse Professional.

The tools I discuss in the chapters ahead are kind of like the tools in my neighbor's garage. Each tool should meet three simple criteria. First, it should be useful. With some basic directions for when and how to safely use it, each tool should have an impact on your life. Second, it should be entertaining. I've tried to include stories that demonstrate the context in which a tool can be used. Frankly, if you don't find a tool entertaining, you are unlikely to use it. Third, it should involve an action step that you can take if you are willing to learn and practice.

One caution: There may not be a single original thought in the pages that follow. I've learned from others and in some cases, have modified a practice. But hopefully my stories, the packaging, and the occasional snarky comment will allow you a new perspective. Sometimes we hear the same advice differently depending on who delivers it and how it is delivered. I hope my delivery will help you.

Chapter 1
Do You Want to Get Well?

The very idea that I am a therapist is hilarious to me. For the first forty years of my life, being a therapist was never an aspiration for me. In fact, if I could have listed twenty-five careers I was likely to pursue, *therapist* wouldn't have been among them. I have had the opportunity to work in some of those twenty-five careers. And there are a few on that list I still would like to try someday.

In an odd sort of way, it was drinking too much and the anger that the drinking fueled that drove me to become a therapist. But any success that I've had has come as a result of the other journeys life has offered me. Some, like working in an ambulance and on the radio, were fun. Others, like loves that came and went, were painful. Yet each one has informed the process which led to this book. In recovery, I have a simple choice every day. Morrie, a great author in his own right, taught that to me first, and others have reminded me often. The choice each day is to add one more day of sobriety, recovery, and serenity, or to go back to zero. And zero sucks. Even for someone who doesn't have an addiction issue, the choice to get better, be better, or live better is new every day.

My Story
When I had finally had enough of my drinking and anger, I reached out to a treatment professional. A very nice lady in treatment had talked to me about the things I'd have to do. "Go to an individual counselor." All right. "Go to a twelve-step meeting."

I stopped her. I said, "You don't understand. I'm here so I won't *have* to go there." I thought I knew about *those* people. I wasn't one of those people, and I didn't want to be with those people or meet those people. I only knew two humans in the entire world who had ever been in a twelve-step meeting. One was a family member; he didn't do very well, so I was pretty sure it didn't work. The other was an old guy called Kenny who went to my church and had spoken about recovery at a banquet talk.

When I went to my first twelve-step meeting, everyone was talking a language I didn't understand. First thing, they rushed up to me and handed me a book. Okay, but I wasn't much of a reader.

Then, they gave me a plastic gold coin, which I thought was weird. They kept looking right at me, like they were talking right at me, and saying, "You've got to get a sponsor."

A sponsor? I thought of a country club. I thought, *No, I'm not going to get a sponsor! It'll cost me money. Besides, I got this.* I left two-thirds of the way through the meeting, completely sure what was going on there was just a bunch of BS. And I did not plan on going back.

Well, there was one itty-bitty mistake in my game plan: Kenny. Kenny and I went to a big church, and that Sunday I just happened to run into him. Is that odd or God? I looked at Kenny and I said, "Hey, I looked into one of those meetings that you talked about in your banquet talk. It sucked, and I left early."

Kenny got this big smile on his face, and he said, "Scott, that's great. I'll come by your house and pick you up today, and we can go to another one in Broad Ripple!" Broad Ripple is at the complete other end of town from where I live. He said, "If you want to leave that one early, you can, but you'll have to walk home."

I did not think that was cool. But Kenny was willing to take me, and the little nice lady in treatment had said I was going to have to go to meetings, so I went to the meeting. Kenny didn't tell me that the meeting on Sunday nights in Broad Ripple lasted an hour and a half. Kenny and I went to the meeting in Broad Ripple, and it didn't kill me. In fact, it was different. Actually, I don't know if *it* was different or if *I* was different. The answer is probably yes. I was with someone whom I trusted, and we stayed for the whole meeting. I met a guy named Rich. I didn't know anything about him. Rich shook my hand; he seemed welcoming but not creepy. Soon, Rich became my sponsor. Rich and I are nothing alike—he's never been married, never had kids. But here's what I know: Rich took me through the steps, and I haven't had to drink or use again since I've had Rich as my sponsor.

I had a choice: to go to that meeting in Broad Ripple or give up on getting better, to get a sponsor or write all of that off as BS. The first and most important realization in recovery is that we do have a choice—on day one, day two, day three and a half, and eleven years and eight days. Every day, we have a choice.

Scott J. Watson

"Do You Want to Get Well?"

There's a story in the Bible, about a dude who sat in the same place for years, right outside a gate by a pool called Bethesda. He sat out there all the time, day in and day out, begging for money with a cup on his mat. Everybody in the town knew him. But one day, a fellow who wasn't from the town walked by—a dude named Jesus. Jesus looked at the fellow with the cup on the mat begging, and he asked him a really interesting question. Jesus didn't say, "Dude, get up. You're not using your life." He didn't say, "Get up. Do something different." Instead, he looked at the beggar on the mat, and he said, "Do you want to get well?"[1]

You could be completely averse to all things Christian; you could have never read the Bible. But for most of us, the question is still valid. Every day, it's appropriate to start our day by answering the question, "Do you want to get well?" I don't know about you, but left to my own devices, I will not drift morally northward. If I wake up and if Scott is doing Scott stuff, I will not drift morally northward. I heard a guy say one time, "If I'm over at your house, and I see something that I want, left to my own devices, I'm probably going to try to steal it. If I'm over at your house, and somebody pisses me off, left to my own devices, I'm probably going to try to fight him. And if I see someone who's hot, left to my own devices, I'm probably going to try to take her to bed." That describes many of us if left to our own devices. Recovery and sponsorship gives us options.

The good news is that we don't have to be left to our own devices. There is a choice that each of us has. We can lie, cheat, and steal; we can let anxiety, depression, shame, guilt, and more win our daily battles. But you have a choice—not your spouse, not your kids, not your boss, not the leader of your homeowner's association or whoever. *You* have a choice. And there's a lot of power in choice.

The choice is really simple: Do I want to get well? Some people are committed to their situations, no matter how bad they are. Am I willing to seek help? Some people are caught up in a victim mentality. Many people are unable or unwilling to change

---

[1] John 5:6, NIV. For the full story from the Bible, see John 5:1-15.

10

because change takes work and can be scary. Am I willing to listen to the suggestions of others? Intimacy with others and spiritual growth are often necessary for change, but many lack the willingness to pursue them. Am I willing to get God? All the texts say it's a spiritual solution. Make sure your God's big enough! The door handle isn't big enough; it's not a Higher Power. You have more power that it does. But even we lack power in the truest sense of the word. We just are not big enough. We have a little power, but not enough to fix ourselves. Our power and our best efforts helped to get us into this mess. When I see someone struggling with God, what I say is, "That's okay. Just keep struggling. Don't quit." I don't care what your God looks like. Just get one. I don't care who your friends are. Just make sure they're real. Are you going to get well? Are you going to get God? And are you going to make friends?

You have a choice today—a choice to use tools that bring you closer to a better life, or to rely on yourself and focus inward toward your problems. And it's a choice you have every day. Every day, you have to answer that question: *Do I want to get well?*

Questions to Consider

1. Growing up, how much choice did you think you had? How did your perception of the power of choice change over time?

2. What does your "God" look like? What experiences have you had with people or churches that have altered your perception of a Higher Power? How is your view of God different than it was when you were ten, twenty, or thirty?

3. What is the most important choice you've made in your effort to have a better life? How did that choice affect you?

4. Today, do you want to get well?

Chapter 2
Three Tough Words

I recently toured a treatment center where I participated in a therapy modality called "The Maze." In the maze, they bring you in blindfolded and allow you to grab hold of a rope, which is wrapped like a web throughout the large room. The rope snakes back and forth from wall to wall and intersects itself many times. They tell you you're in a maze and then offer only one bit of instruction: "If you think you've found the way out or if you need something, you should raise your hand."

So I'm walking in the maze. I'm trying to find my way out and minding my own business like I always do. I figure that I'm fairly smart and very competitive, so I'm sure I'll find my way out. All of a sudden, I feel something different and I think I've found the way out. I raise my hand. An attendant comes over and I say, "I think I found my way out!"

The guide says, "No."

And every few minutes, all of us who are in this maze are told, "If you think you've found the way out or if you need something, raise your hand."

I keep walking, reaching, feeling, and thinking. Six times I raise my hand because I think I've found the way out and every time: "No. But if you think you've found a way out or if you need something, raise your hand." This goes on for about twenty-five minutes.

At some point, somebody says, "Congratulations to Stephen; he's found the way out!" They're all clapping and I think, *Man, I'm smarter than Stephen. I'm younger, fitter, and cooler.* A few minutes later: "Congratulations, Sheila found her way out." I'm getting angry. I think, *I'm way fitter than Sheila! What is going on?*

Every few minutes, someone keeps saying, "If you think you've found your way out or need something, raise your hand." I think, *What am I missing here? What did they find or what do they know that I am missing?*

Have you ever wondered that when you look at the people around you? Has it ever felt like other folks have "the secret of life" that they are not willing to share with you? Have you ever been baffled by others who just seem so comfortable in their own skin?

After many failed attempts and probably forty minutes in the maze, it dawned on me: The six people who found their way out didn't do it because they were smarter, faster, luckier, or trickier than me. They found their way out because they raised their hands and asked for help.

"I Need Help"

Growing up, we hear many mixed messages about asking for help. As a child, I was confused when I sang, "No man is an island, no man stands alone. Each man's joy is joy to me; each man's pain is my own,"[2] and the very next day heard sayings like, "Pull yourself up by your boot straps," "God helps those who help themselves," and the always encouraging "You got yourself into this mess; you need to get yourself out." As a child, it was never clear to me whose responsibility it was to get me out of the predicaments I faced in life. As an adult, I'm still not always sure.

I've heard it said that "I love you" are the hardest three words to say. This may well be true for a great many people. Maybe you want more than anything else for Mom or Dad to look you in the eyes and say, "I love you." Maybe you have longed for a boyfriend or girlfriend to either tell you or show you that they love you. Or perhaps it's your spouse who promised "for better or worse" but whose words or actions do not express it. That's a *big deal*. I know that as a therapist, but I want to suggest to you that "I love you" are not the three toughest words in life. The three toughest words to say are, "I need help."

The truth is every one of us has been locked in a maze at some point in our lives. The maze can look like an addiction, money problems, grief, loss, business decisions, educational struggles, infidelity, shame, or anything else that causes you to lose sleep, curse at God, or doubt yourself. Books, poems, and song

---

[2] Joan Baez, "No Man Is an Island," lines 1-4.

lyrics all remind us that asking for help can be tough. The lyrics *"There is none so blind as he who will not see"*[3] can crash against the Alcoholics Anonymous saying, *"He is an extreme example of self-will run riot, though he usually does not think so."* What's left is a picture of you or me surrounded by people who would be willing to help if only we would reach out our hands and ask. It is hard to ask for help.

Barriers to Asking for Help

Stephen, a twenty-six-year-old man, calls to inquire about the cost of getting a substance-use evaluation. He drives a delivery van for a small company and was charged with a DUI while driving home from a high-school reunion. He is honest with his employer, who tells him that he's a great employee and they don't want to lose him. He needs the evaluation to keep his job but he can't afford to pay for it. Without help, he will likely lose his job. But Stephen won't ask his folks for help because he's "on his own" financially and doesn't want to be honest about the DUI.

Shelly is a woman with three young children who occupy nearly all of her time. She is able to work one or two days each week delivering mail. She is married to a man who is both abusive and an angry drug addict. She cries every day because she wants to get away from her husband, but the income from her job isn't much. She worries that he will find her and harm her or their children. She feels trapped and frozen. She hates what her life has become but fears that if she were to leave, things would only get worse. So she endures the beatings, name calling, and manipulation from her addicted husband. Without help, Shelly may lose her life. The kids may lose their mom. But Shelly won't talk to her parents because they have never liked her husband. Shelly fears they will say, "We told you so," should she explain the situation fully.

Both Stephen and Shelly are afraid to ask for help, afraid of how their families and friends might react if they admit they need it. They are afraid of criticism, afraid of admitting that they have landed in a predicament they cannot escape on their own. Maybe

---

[3] Johnny Mathis and Ray Stevens, "Everything Is Beautiful"

they won't ask for help because they do not feel they deserve it. When pressed on this, they may argue their points. They may cite any number of reasons for their hesitation, all the while feeling like they are not worth being helped. Or maybe they won't ask for help because they feel they are burdens to their friends and families. They may think the people they could ask for help "already have a lot on their plates," "have got a lot going on," "are on fixed incomes," or "have a kid in college." Do any of these excuses sound familiar? When was the last time you asked for help?

If I were to pick up the phone and call all the people whom you might ask for help, is there one person who would say, "He or she is really not worth it"? Is there one person who would say, "It's too much of a burden" or, "They don't deserve my help"? The answer is *no*! I work with families of addicts all the time, and they say to me, "Just save my kid's life. Save my spouse's life. I'll do whatever it takes, even if I don't have the money."

I'm lousy at asking for help, but I'm getting better. When you fail to ask somebody for help while you are in life's maze, you deny somebody the opportunity to be of service to you. It's not about you, about your pride, your ego. You're responsible for your part of the deal—asking. They're responsible for whether or not they're able or willing to help you—that's their part of the deal. Your willingness to ask for help is totally up to you; their willingness and ability to help is up to them. Don't get those mixed up. You want to honor your friends? Ask them for help. You want to respect whatever your friends have got on their plates? Let them know they have the option to say no. You want to feel great when someone helps you? Then make the most of the experience or opportunity. It's that simple.

Recently, I knew someone whose aunt needed a place to stay when fire damaged her house. The aunt didn't want to ask for help for fear that her presence would be a bother. Repairs on her house were likely to take several months, and the insurance company's response was less than the family had hoped for. The client had talked with her husband, and together, they agreed to allow the aunt to live in their basement. What resulted was a wonderful relationship, where the aunt helped around the house and was a blessing to have around. While my client was happy to have her basement back, she reported that there were tears when the aunt finally went "home." Ask for help. Say, "I need help." You cannot get out of the maze alone.

Questions to Consider

1. Have you ever been in a maze—physically, mentally, financially, or relationally—that you could not get out of without help? Did you ask for help?

2. Why do you think it is so hard to ask for help? What messages did you hear about asking for help when you were growing up?

3. What barriers keep you from asking for help?

4. When was the last time someone asked *you* for help? How did it make you feel?

Chapter 3
Life Is a Team Sport

Del's Story

Have you ever had a kidney stone? I have! When I'm speaking, I will often ask for a show of hands and then ask, "Did you think you were dying?" Most folks say it was the worst pain they had ever experienced. Some folks say that they didn't think they were dying, but that the pain was so bad they hoped they would.

Del was a guy who called everybody "dude." So when my phone rang one evening at about 8:40 p.m. and I saw it was Del, I picked the phone up and said, "Dude," before he could.

"Dude," Del said, "what's it like to have a kidney stone?"

Unfortunately, I was overly qualified to answer the question. "Well, dude, it sucks," I said. "Sometimes your back hurts. Sometimes your groin hurts. Sometimes you pee blood. You might as well head for the ER, because you're not going to get through this without some pain medicine." (You know it's bad when the addiction counselor suggests pain medicine.)

After I explained the pain in the flank, groin, and gut; the nausea, vomiting, and blood in the urine; and the difference between dull pain and the waves of pain that would accompany a kidney stone, Del said: "I've got a kidney stone."

I assured him that it was going to be a bumpy few hours. I suggested he find out exactly where and how big the stone was. Our conversation ended with me laughing because another had joined the ranks of the stone prone. "Call me tomorrow and let me know how you're doing," I said.

The next morning at 10 a.m., Del called again. I picked it up. "Dude, how's the kidney stone?"

Del's words and his tone of voice are something I will never forget. "Scott," he said, "I so wish I had a kidney stone." He proceeded to tell me that the ER doctors had found a tumor about the size of a football on his kidney. I was shocked. "They're going to take my kidney tomorrow. They said I got cancer; it's bad."

17

"Man, I'm so sorry." I didn't know what else to say.

Del wasn't my best friend. Rather, he was a member of a large group of people I had come to know in the preceding five years. I knew most of them fairly well, but while we were close as a group, most of us were not close as individuals. All of that was about to change.

I started making some phone calls. Our group had a T-shirt made for Del. On the front, it said *DUDE* in big letters, and on the back, it said, *Where's my kidney?* We gave it to the nurse to put on him in the recovery room, so that when he woke up from surgery, he would have it on. Thus began several months of our group of friends doing things for Del. We mowed the grass, took him to doctor's appointments, and did whatever we could. Del began an aggressive course of chemotherapy, and at first he tolerated it pretty well.

One day in the fall, he called and asked, "What are you doing the rest of the day?"

I said, "Nothing that can't be cancelled."

"Well, Allan is a freshman; he has his first freshman tennis match today. Is there any way you could get me over there so I could watch my son play tennis?"

He was asking for help. And I was going to move heaven and earth so that this guy with cancer could get to his kid's first freshman tennis match. I arrived at Del's house and moved both Del and his wheelchair into the car. We drove to the tennis courts, and of course his kid was playing on a court on the other side of the building. I pushed Del over there and locked the wheels of his chair in. I put some sunscreen on him, and we watched as his son got shredded 6-0. Allan didn't win a game, but he did have a huge smile on his face when he noticed that his dad was there to watch. I helped Del back in the car and dropped him off at his home just as somebody else from our group was bringing the family dinner.

This went on day after day and week after week—chemo, doctor's appointments, tennis matches, twelve-step meetings, meals, prayers, and the whole deal. One Saturday the first week of December, we got an e-mail from Mike, one of the members in our group, that said, "We're going to clean up Del's house and clear the gutters; we're going to rake the leaves; we're going to get the house ready for winter." So on a cold morning, about twenty-five of us showed up at Del's house with trash bags and power tools. We clipped bushes, cleaned gutters, cut grass, and bagged garbage. We got everything out to the street and ate some Subway sandwiches that Del's wife provided for us.

Most of the guys took off after that, and two or three of us lingered as Julie, Del's wife, came in. Then she asked for help. She looked at us and said, "Before you guys go, could you run up in the attic and bring down the Christmas decorations? That was always Del's job, and we want to try to decorate the house for Christmas." So Mike and I climbed up and handed down Christmas decorations.

Del's cancer was spreading. He was losing weight, and our group was worried. Each Friday at noon, several of us would gather with Del for an hour. Our odd little group had first met because we drank, drugged, ate, or raged in such a way that our relationships with others were damaged. But now through Del's ordeal we were building relationships with each other. We were told that hour was his favorite hour of the week, and it was special for each of us as well. Del was rehospitalized for difficulty breathing and pain management. Because of the challenges, it was decided that Del should not be left alone. So for several weeks members of our now expanding group agreed to hang out with Del 24/7. It was remarkable, really. Men and women who knew each other but were not close all agreed to help a friend and his family. In the process, we got to know each other better and we met others who would become our closest friends.

One day when I was just walking into the 11 a.m. service at my church, I noticed Del's wife was calling me. I stepped out and took the call. "Scott, Del has taken a turn for the worse overnight. He's on oxygen and not able to speak. It doesn't look good," Julie said. I expressed my sadness but was not ready for what would follow. "We've always told the kids that if they prayed and if Del continued with his treatments, then Daddy would get better. The truth is, Del's in ICU on a lot of oxygen; he may not make it through the day. Would you please come and tell the kids?"

I agreed. I asked my wife and my neighbor who sits in front of me in church, "Can you pray for me? I'm about to do something really hard." I couldn't believe it. I was thinking, *When I decided to stop drinking, I did not sign up for telling a man's children that he was going to die. That's not what I was trying to do when I came to that first twelve-step meeting with Kenny.*

It was a long and lonely drive to the other side of town. When I got to Del's house, his young daughter, Sally, was sitting on the hospital bed in the living room next to her cat. I was afraid. There is no good way to explain to a fifteen-year-old son and a nine-year-old daughter that their father and hero is about to die. I looked at little Sally and I said, "Sally, your dad who I know is your hero is really, really sick. We've all been praying that he's going to get better. The truth is, Daddy's probably not going to get better. In fact, he could die very soon. But your dad's fought hard. Your dad's going to die sober, and that was important to him. And your dad has got somebody from his group with him twenty-four hours a day. We love him, too. He has taught us a lot, and we are very sad".

Let's be honest. That moment was really heavy. It was one of the hardest things I have ever done. There were a lot of tears. After that, Allan came in, and we had a similar conversation. Allan was angry and frustrated; he didn't want to believe that his dad, a triathlete who had once seemed so strong and invincible, now had met his match in cancer. I went home and I just collapsed under the weight of what I'd done. Never would I have guessed that being a friend would include tasks like that.

About three days later, I visited Del in his hospital room. He was sedated, and there was a large oxygen mask over his face. As was the custom, he had someone from our group staying with him. Robert was with us and he was much newer to our group. I didn't know Robert well. We had been together for a few group meals, and he seemed aloof. He wasn't fun, and I didn't care to get to know him. Robert was seated in a chair on the far side of Del's bed, and I sat next to Del in the chair nearest the door.

After a while, Del's eyes opened. With great effort, he shifted onto his right side and looked my way with those steely eyes. "Tell me about my kids," he demanded.

At first I could not tell if Del was angry, grateful, or merely curious. I placed my hand on him, and we both cried as I relayed how I had told his two children about his eventual fate. In that moment, I felt a strange mix of torture, torment, grief, fear, accomplishment, honor, and pride. It was clear that Del was grateful for my efforts. It was also one of the most emotional, gut-wrenching conversations that I have ever been part of. I would never have willingly signed up to cry so hard and hurt so much, yet at the same time, I wouldn't have missed it for the entire world.

As the tears slowed, I looked over and saw Robert. Here was a guy who agreed to stay with a dying man whom he didn't know well. Instead of just sitting quietly and reading, Robert had been "hostage" to a weighty conversation. As Del drifted back to sleep, I called Robert out into the hallway. We hugged, and I apologized as I acknowledged that when he signed up to sit with Del, he likely didn't sign up for that much emotion either. He, too, was moved by the gravity of the situation. As a result of that shared experience with Del, Robert has grown to be one of my closest friends. We have dined, golfed, travelled, talked, and done what good friends do. We call each other for advice and help. Recently, Robert was married, and I was honored to be included in the wedding party.

That afternoon was also the first time that Del and I discussed his dying. Prior to that, our conversations had focused on his treatment and the hope of healing. Del indicated that dying didn't scare him. He was worried about how the kids would do without a dad. With the truth before us, I made Del an offer. If he would like, I would bring recording equipment to the hospital so that he could tape messages for his kids, wife, and friends. Initially, he balked. However, a few days later his wife called and said Del was ready to take me up on whatever the offer was I had made him. She asked me if she wanted to know what it was. I told her it was Del's to tell and not mine.

Over the next several days, Del got stronger, and we sat together and recorded his final messages to his family and friends. Each was heartfelt and exacted an emotional toll on both of us. I carefully clarified with him how each message was to be used. He decided that the unedited master tape would go to his wife alone. This would allow her to hear the context in which each conversation took place. Edited copies of his words were given to each child and a few others as he directed.

Del died about three weeks later. The group that had been with him on Fridays at noon was joined by many others at the funeral. Several of his closest friends spoke about how, in dying, Del had brought people together. I looked over at Robert and wiped a tear.

One of the messages that Del recorded was a final farewell to his little tribe of friends who had driven, cleaned, visited, supported, read, talked, and cried with him over the many months of his illness, and who had eventually carried him to a final resting place. That message was to be played one time only on the Wednesday after his death. His wife and close friends joined for the playing of a tape that expressed Del's love, thanks, hope, and gratitude. Del had a team, a team to comfort, encourage, and help him through that painful period of illness and eventual death. Del's team sought to support him and his family through all of the obstacles that living with cancer offered. We all need a team like that.

Your Team

A friend of mine often says, "You can't pick your parents and you can't pick your kids, but you'd better pick a team." To succeed in tough times, you have to pick a team. Your team does not include your family. Family is family, something they sign on to until death or divorce. Coworkers aren't your team either. They are your coworkers. At this point, you may be asking, "Who does that leave?"

The truth may be that you don't *have* a team. If so, you *need* one. Begin to recruit one. A team is a group of friends who sign on to do all of life with you. That doesn't mean that there are no boundaries. In fact, the best team members have the best boundaries. Whom would you call in the middle of the night if the person closest to you were to die? Who in your life would be upset if you *didn't* call him or her? Who are the people you can best depend on for honest advice? You want a team with presence, with proximity, and with honesty.

Lee was a guy who attended our noon-time group only twice a month. He lived in New York but was in our city on business regularly. One day, Lee looked at us and said, "Now, it's been sixteen years. It's not really practical for me to meet daily with my team for ninety days, especially with my travel schedule, but you know what? I can call ninety *people* in ninety days."

A small group of us made eye contact. It was as if Lee was speaking to our souls. That was in 2004. Since then, that little band of us has rarely missed a day calling each other.

Ralph will call me and say, "When are you going to be back in town? Let's do lunch on Friday."

I'll say, "I don't usually work on Friday; I'm seeing a client on Friday."

He'll say, "What time do you have—what time is breakfast that week?"

When you talk with your team, it doesn't always have to be about how you're struggling or how you need help. You can just talk about life. The point is that you are doing something. If Ralph and I are friends, and we start calling each other every day and talking about nothing, then when something's going on in one of our lives, it's going to be a lot easier to pick up the phone and talk about something serious. But if we don't talk for ten days, it seems harder to pick up the phone and talk. Life's a team sport. Recovery from addiction, grief, shame, and trauma is a team sport. All of these things try and demand to stay hidden and buried. But when that happens, there is no healing. We just stay sick or get sicker.

Some people say, "I'm an introvert; people wear me out." I don't care. Life's a team sport; you can be an introvert and still have friends. The secret is to know and to be known. There are plenty of introverts with a few close friends. Building these relationships involves risk. But my experience, both personally and professionally, is that when someone knows my secrets and is still willing to take my calls or meet me for breakfast, there is no better feeling.

Here is the problem: If you don't have a team, you're screwed. You can't pick your parents. You can't pick your kids. But you had better pick your team. Only a fool would believe that there will never come a time when your world turns upside down.

Perhaps, like Del, you will receive a challenging diagnosis. Perhaps the news will not be medical at all. Divorce papers, arrest warrants, death notifications, financial turmoil, and job loss can all disrupt our lives. The ability to find balance and think clearly may well be determined by the team that is in place to help you cope with the challenges of life. In the strongest words possible, I want to urge—no, beg—you to begin picking a team.

Questions to Consider

1. Think of someone you know who has a great team. What are some of the characteristics of that team?

2. What kinds of people do you want on your team? How would you define a good teammate?

3. Which people in your life might make great teammates? Write down a list of those people. Would anybody say that you are on their team?

4. How can you start to "do life with" the people on your list this week?

Chapter 4
That's Just Perfect

Life is best when it's not lived alone; it is best when you pick a team. It can be hard to have a team. In a team, you have to be honest, but for those of us who are *perfectionists*, that can be painfully difficult.

I must admit that while I appreciate and at times demand good quality, my lack of attention to detail will never lead anyone to accuse me of being a perfectionist. Still, when I travel to speak to groups and ask about perfectionism, about ten to fifteen percent of people identify as perfectionists.

What's so wrong with perfectionism? After all, isn't it good to want things to be just right? Maybe you have high standards and don't expect anything of others that you don't also demand of yourself.

The Problem of Perfectionism
The University of Illinois Center for Counseling suggests that perfectionism can have its beginning in one of several places:

- fear of failure;
- fear of making mistakes;
- fear of disapproval;
- all-or-none thinking;
- overemphasis on "shoulds"; and
- believing that others are easily successful.[4]

The first three origins of perfectionism identify it as something that stems from fear. This means that all too often the goal of perfectionism isn't really getting something right. Instead, the goal of perfectionism is to avoid negative feelings or messages. A negative message might be, "I'm not good enough," "I don't

---

[4] "Perfectionism," *University of Illinois Counseling Center* (Board of Trustees of the University of Illinois, 2007), www.counselingcenter.illinois.edu/self-help-brochures/academic-difficulties/perfectionism.

measure up," "I'm a failure," "I'm a disappointment," "I don't matter," "I'm not worthy," or "I don't deserve this." This is called *shame*. In all of us, the desire to avoid a painful message is unbelievably strong; perfectionists are generally not aware that this is what drives their efforts. They will justify perfectionism any number of ways, but despite their pleadings and protestations, it is the fear of a painful message that drives their desires to be perfect. What they don't realize—and what many of us who have sought to avoid these messages have not realized—is that these negative messages are lies. When viewed through the lens of a friend or Higher Power, these negative messages simply are not the truth.

The fourth origin on the list deals with all-or-none thinking. I find myself slipping into this kind of thinking from time to time. It carries with it its own set of challenges.

The all-or-none thinker tends to view life in a concrete way. Life is a series of good/bad, yes/no, right/wrong, nice/mean, generous/greedy decisions about people and events. The evidence (or at least some of it) is gathered, and a decision is made. Based on that decision, another is made. The problem is that this mind-set involves a great deal of *judgment*. This places the perfectionist at the center of every situation, where he or she can judge the acceptable standard or quality of others' efforts.

Judgment is also at the center of people who have a lot of "shoulds" in their lives. I have a friend who has a very challenging relationship with her mother. When she was a child, her mother was unavailable both physically and emotionally. Her mother would frequently belittle her. When they are together, her mother is still very critical; yet my friend feels terribly guilty if she doesn't call her mother every day.

I'm not sure where I first heard the phrase, but the best advice for perfectionists who live by the code of what should and should not be done is this: *Don't should all over yourself.* Say it out loud quickly if it didn't make sense when you read it.

The final origin on this list is the belief that others succeed easily. This, too, involves a mix of fear and judgment. Perfectionists fear that for the same amount of work and effort, they won't get as much reward or credit as other people. This perpetuates the painful message that "I'm not as good as someone." Concern builds that somehow the field of life is unbalanced in someone else's favor. This of course isn't usually true. One of the key ways to uncover and avoid this myth is to be careful where our focus lies. If I focus is on what I don't have or what someone else does have, then I won't be grateful for what I *do* have. The truth is that comparing yourself to another is almost never helpful.

We Are Human

Leon was a guy whom I got to know pretty well. One of the things I admired about him was his seeming ability to not judge others harshly. When he encountered people who were perfectionists and judged themselves or others harshly, Leon would always say something like, "It's hard being human!" Indeed there are times when it is hard to be human. But it is even tougher for people *not* to be human.

Humans are what we are. There is no way for us *not* to be human. Leon used to remind folks that no amount of therapy, no prayer, nor all the self-help books in the world could combine to change one immutable law: We are *always* going to be human.

If you are a perfectionist, I want you to take a deep breath and sit back before reading the rest of this paragraph. The fundamental, unchangeable, and irrefutable truth is that being flawed is a critical element of being human. That's right. The fact that you *are* human means, among other things, that you *are not* perfect. It also means that you are going to make mistakes. Perfectionists seek not to make any mistakes. Their goal is to be perfect on projects at work and in relationships with others. Perfectionists seek to be something that is impossible. That is a losing game; and sometimes, when perfectionists begin to sense that they are losing, they will redouble their efforts and try harder. This just leads to more frustration, more feelings that they are "not doing it right" or "aren't good enough," more painful messages that we try desperately to avoid.

As I've said, when I speak to audiences, I like to ask perfectionists to raise their hands. Once they self-identify, I like to ask them to keep their hands up if they believe there is a God. In a typical crowd, only one or two hands will lower at this point. Then I wade into water that is uncomfortable to some.

Let's be clear about one thing: I'm no expert on theology or world religions. However, my understanding of most religions is that each one has a framework to deal with the fact that we are not perfect. The Christian faith is the framework that I am most familiar with, because in addition to my trying to practice it, it has historically informed many of the decisions made in Western cultures and governments.

The concepts of grace and forgiveness are predicated on the fact that you and I are flawed. If I never make a mistake, then I never need to be forgiven. If I never have expectations, defects, flaws, or shortcomings, then there is no need for me to forgive you. There's a book I read from time to time that backs me up on this: "All have sinned and fall short of the glory of God" (Romans 3:23, NIV).

If this is the case, then how is it possible to be a perfectionist and to grow one's faith, without it taking a huge toll on one's psyche? Perfectionism exacts an *enormous* toll on both the psychological and spiritual well-beings of those who subscribe to it.

The image that comes to mind is this. Imagine that you are walking all the way across the airport to your next gate. As you walk, you spot a conveyor belt. You are excited because you believe the conveyor belt will get you to the new gate quicker and with less effort. Your luggage is checked, so all that you have to manage is yourself and your carry-on bag.

About twenty seconds after you step onto the belt, it occurs to you that it's going in reverse. Instead of helping you get to your destination more quickly, it's actually working like a treadmill. You are strong and in a hurry. So you decide to walk faster and faster, only to have the belt speed up too. You begin to feel irritated so you go even faster; the treadmill pace quickens. Furious over the wasted energy and time, you relent and allow the treadmill to take you back to the place where your ill-fated journey began. You agree to just accept that the conveyor was not what you believed it to be. So you step to the side and begin to walk to your gate.

28

Chasing the goal of perfection wears people out. Perfectionists are stuck on a treadmill but have no control over its pace. This results in attempt after attempt to manipulate and control circumstances, often in an effort to avoid painful messages. The result, however, is even more pain, resentment, anger, and frustration. Relationships become strained, and when the dust settles, the same choices remain.

One tool for countering perfectionism is to be honest. There is a church near Chicago that I admire. In 2002, they did a sermon series called "28 Days of Truth-telling." The deal was to try to go twenty-eight days without telling a lie. My recollection is that the average person made it six and a half days. They were churchgoers. But they are human too.

We humans have a hard time telling the truth all the time. We're not always hardwired for the truth, so we have to work at it. It is an acquired skill. We *need* to learn to tell the truth to ourselves and to others. Sometimes we need to rely on others who can see the truth about us more clearly than we can. Only when we are honest can we face perfectionism and pick a real team, a team that knows our true selves, not our "perfect," fake selves.[5]

Questions to Consider

1. Are you a perfectionist? Why or why not?

2. Which of the sources of perfectionism listed by the University of Illinois Counseling Center do you most identify with? Explain.

3. How does the fact that you are (and always will be) human affect the way you judge yourself and others?

4. What do you think your life would look like if you set aside the burden of perfectionism and engaged in truthful relationships?

5. What is the one hurtful message about yourself that you seek to avoid? Are you able to spot the lie in the message?

---

[5] This has been addressed quite well by others including Ernie Kurtz in his book, *Not God,* and by Stephanie E. in her wonderful publication *Shame Faced.*

Chapter 5
Rearview Mirrors

My grandfather used to drive an old truck with a skinny, little stick shift. I loved everything about that truck. It was a turquoise color with a round top that looked like a turtle shell. It had hard, plastic mesh seats that were striped in many colors but just looked dark from a distance. After a while, he traded that truck for a station wagon; it was a crème color and lacked excitement except for two things.

First, it had what he called a "gate," which was the car version of a tailgate that he would flip down. Sometimes he would allow me to ride on it from the metal barn where the horses and tools were kept to the pond where I fished and learned how to row a boat. Every time I was on that tailgate, I felt both cool and terrified. Perhaps I lacked adventure as a youth. Second, the car had a small mirror attached to the front windshield. My grandfather told me that when he looked in that, he could see what was happening behind him. It was the first time I had ever been aware of a rearview mirror.

Several years ago, I heard my friend and mentor Morrie say, "Rearview mirrors are useful, but not for navigation." When I first heard that, I thought, *duh*! But with time, I've come to realize the implications of that little phrase are huge. When driving a car, we are taught to scan the rearview mirror along with the mirrors on each side of the car; however, we do not navigate by using a rearview mirror. When I became a therapist, I was surprised by the number of clients who were navigating their futures by looking at their pasts. Morrie's lesson was not about our driving, but about our lives. The stuff in our past—our rearview mirrors—can be useful. Our pasts can provide insights about why we are who we are and about the patterns of our behaviors; our pasts can even help us avoid making the same mistakes again. Our pasts can *inform* our futures, but they are not reliable tools for navigating the future. If you spend your whole life looking at what you've done or what was done to you, you'll wreck.

Stuck in the Rearview Mirror

Tina grew up in a loving home where she was several years younger than her siblings. She said she was always lonely. Her parents divorced when Tina was eight, and as the youngest, she never felt like either parent had much time for her. She battled weight problems and didn't date much through high school. Shortly before graduation, Tina was invited to a church that seemed loving but "different."

Tina had not been to church while growing up, but that summer after she graduated high school was her best ever. She enjoyed being with other people her age, especially boys. The church only allowed you to date and marry other church members. The elders of the church did not arrange for marriages but they played some role in spouse selection. Tina was fine with this; she hadn't been dating at all and for the first time in her life she felt like she belonged. She enjoyed being with her new friends, one of which was Tony, a young man who seemed to like her.

In time, Tony and Tina began dating, though often in a group. The summer passed quickly, and all too soon Tina went a short distance away to college. Many weekends Tina would come back to be with her new friends and with Tony. Hers and Tony's relationship progressed nicely, and she felt sure that the church elders supported their union. However, one weekend when Tina returned, Tony had an announcement to make to their group of friends. He had gone to the church leaders and asked to be married to Tina's close friend.

Tina was devastated. She dropped out of the church. Then she dropped out of school. All she could think about was Tony and the fact that he had chosen someone else. She lived with a deep feeling of loneliness, which had been her constant companion as a child. After a while, Tina began dating again. It was an uncomfortable experience, and she feared rejection at every turn. In time, she met and married a man who was far better than she believed she deserved. In fact, she reports that she still sometimes wonders if he is going to abandon her. When she discusses this with him, he tries to reassure her. Still, she doubts. While her marriage is good, she says she still thinks about Tony every week. She hears stories from her hometown about how successful he is and what a good athlete his son is. In short, even though she is happily married to another man, she is still a slave to her past.

Danny was a guy whom I didn't know well. We had a number of mutual friends, and he managed a business that I frequent. When he was diagnosed with cancer, I began to take more of an interest in his well-being, but though I admired his customer service and management style, we were never close.

But when I attended Danny's funeral, I was struck by something. Although he died in his midfifties, nearly every reference made at his funeral was to his military service which ended at age twenty-five. It was as if there was nothing noteworthy to mention from the last thirty years of Danny's life.

Don't get me wrong. The military service of Danny and all veterans is important, but one risk of focusing on the past is missing out on the opportunities of today. The efforts of those brave men shaped this country and allowed us the freedom that we enjoy today, but life and service to others does not end with an honorable discharge. There was sadness in me as I left the memorial service, that Danny had left a lot of life on the table. Were there opportunities in those last thirty years that Danny failed to seize?

Some folks live in their pasts not because of their successful achievements but rather because their pasts were traumatic. It's not uncommon to feel chained to the past—whether because of past success, because you did something you weren't proud of, or because something unspeakably traumatic was done to you. In all cases, people suffer needlessly when they hang onto times that no longer serve them and that cloud their view of the possibilities for a brighter today.

Right Here, Right Now

The stuff in your rearview mirror is history. It's important; it might even be noteworthy, but it is your past and not your future. Perhaps you've heard the saying, "If I've got one foot in yesterday and another in tomorrow, I'm pooping all over today." Every morning when you get up, you have a choice about what you will make of today. Yesterday doesn't matter. Keep your head where your butt is: right here, right now. I don't know what you're worried about right now, but I'll guarantee it is about stuff in the past or stuff in the future, because right here right now you're okay.

What are you doing today that would be worthy of mention at your funeral? Whom have you called on, written to, or helped so far this week? What are you doing in your family, community, workplace, neighborhood, or church that will leave a better life for others? If the answers to these questions are troubling to you, take heart! There is still time. I don't care if your rearview mirror is dirty or crystal clear; it is not useful for navigation. You do not have to be a slave to your past, to its shame or to its honor. You have work to do right here and right now.

Questions to Consider

1. If rearview mirrors are not useful for navigation, then what are they useful for? How can you acknowledge the stuff in your past without letting it dictate your future?

2. What things in your past tend to get you stuck looking in your rearview mirror? What past hurts, regrets, or accomplishments discourage you from making the most of today? What would it take for you to tell somebody you trust about these barriers, so that you could better enjoy today?

3. How does the revelation that "right here right now you're okay" impact the way you view today?

4. Think about the questions asked in this chapter: What are you doing today that would be worthy of mention at your funeral? Whom have you called on, written to, or helped so far this week? What are you doing in your family, community, workplace, or church that will leave a better life for others? If you don't like your answers to these questions, what can you do to change them? How much longer are you willing to wait?

Chapter 6
Crystal Balls

"Yesterday (the stuff in your rearview mirror) is history. Tomorrow (the stuff in your crystal ball) is a mystery. Today is a gift; that's why they call it the present." This saying has been around a long time, but it feels like a fitting way to begin this chapter.

When my friend Del was dying of cancer, he and I had a number of emotional conversations. One afternoon I was sitting with him in hospice, and we knew he only had a few days left. I asked him a question he had often asked me, "Dude, what have you learned through all of this?"

He said, "I've learned that my crystal ball is broken."

"I'm sorry."

"It's not like that," Del said. "I thought my life was going to end with me and Julie retiring to Florida. I'd play golf, she'd have a boutique, and we'd have grandkids and all of that. I guess my crystal ball has been broken since the day I was born. I thought I'd run the world. Julie would say, 'Our parents are coming this weekend,' and my crystal ball would think, *Oh no, the in-laws are coming for the entire weekend. This is going to be bad!* But on Monday morning, I'd wake up and realize I'd had a pretty good weekend. I never get to play golf on Saturday except when my father-in-law is in town. On Saturday night, Julie's parents stayed with the kids so Julie and I actually got to go out and have dinner together as adults on a date. What I thought was going to be the worst weekend ever would actually turn out to be pretty cool."

Del dreaded the in-laws coming until they actually made the weekend better. He was a triathlete until the day he thought he had a kidney stone but learned instead it was cancer. Life doesn't play out like we see it in our crystal balls. I don't know what your crystal ball says about your job, marriage, kids, health, wealth, or the future, but let me just suggest to you that your crystal ball is just as broken as Del's was and mine is.

My Crystal Ball Story

The morning I started my job as the Central Indiana Director of a large company, I woke up well before my alarm clock went off and headed to the shower. I left the house wearing a starched white shirt with a new tie and my favorite dark suit that I had gotten when my grandmother died. I looked the part and was ready to conquer the world from my office with a view.

After being unemployed or underemployed for many months, it was time to start my new job; and while I wasn't the CEO, I was the Central Indiana Director! That meant the biggest territory, a nice office, a generous salary, and a future that was finally what I thought I deserved. I would have lots of flexibility, exciting projects to make happen, and the opportunity to turn an underperforming area into a financial juggernaut. My life was finally looking up, and my new job was going to be a key component in my awesome future.

Things started off quite well. I loved the freedom that came with being the boss. The work itself was kind of boring, but I was able to stay motivated. The Executive Director was my boss, but she seemed rather detached and unaware of what was going on. When decisions needed to be made, she relied on the Board of Directors and "volunteers" who were the backbone of the organization. What's more, it was frustrating that my new secretary couldn't type a one-page letter without an error.

But these were only minor setbacks. Away from the office, I was buying toys, eating out, traveling a little, playing golf, and dating. My new apartment was nothing fancy, but it was in a great neighborhood close to friends, family, tennis, bars, and outdoor recreation. Life was great, and it was all because I had the best job in the world.

In fairly short order, things at work began to change. The secretary who couldn't type also turned out to be a little rude on the phone and a lot lazy. She couldn't keep a secret and only showed up for work about 85 percent of the time. There were fundraising goals which we met, but the Executive Director wasn't too excited about the hard work needed to achieve them and wasn't used to working with younger people. The volunteers ended up being folks who suggested how things could be changed but never seemed available to implement those ideas. In short, I wasn't enjoying my new title, important office, or those with whom I worked.

The productivity of the Central Indiana area was greater than all of the other territories combined. We were setting records. It was clear early on that my boss, who was forty years older than me, didn't like me personally. It seemed like she was only willing to put up with me because I was making her look really good.

About a year after I started, I was called into her office. After a long lecture in which she didn't say too much that caught my attention, she asked me to resign. *That* captured my attention. Because I didn't think she had the guts to fire me I looked at her and said, "No way!"

She reached under her desk and pulled out a box which she handed to me as she fired me. "Peter will watch you clean out your office. You can give your key to him."

In less than fourteen months, this wonderful job which was the key to my future was gone. I remember sitting in the parking lot and wondering just how a job which held so much promise could vaporize. That job was my ticket to so many great things, and yet I never really enjoyed working there. The flood of emotions and thoughts was overwhelming as I pulled out of the parking lot for the final time. But I was crystal clear about one thing: That job was *not* what I expected. In my crystal ball, it had been the key to my future. In reality, it felt like another dead end. My crystal ball had failed me.

All of us have relied heavily on a defective crystal ball at one point or another, and all of us have stories. Perhaps you were disappointed by your first spouse. Perhaps, like Del, a difficult diagnosis or tragic event altered what you could reasonably expect in your life. One could argue that such off-time events are the exception rather than the rule, but even so, they demonstrate how important it is to simply live in the present moment.

Crystal balls can work both ways. There are many people who would tell you that their greatest gifts or blessings came when early returns did not look favorable. I know a man who has been happily married for twenty-seven years. He and his wife are quick to report that, for the first two months they knew each other, they didn't like each other. Nevertheless, they began to date, and obviously those impressions changed.

There are stories of employees worrying about policy changes and promotion strategies who say, "I'd quit before I'd work for that person"—until they are promoted and their bosses turn out to be wonderful supervisors. Redemption, open-mindedness, and acceptance can work together to make even the most difficult situations bearable.

Sometimes crystal balls fuel worry. The Tuesday before my oldest son, The Goose, was scheduled to have his wisdom teeth removed, I asked him, "Are you nervous?"

"No...should I be?" he asked.

I said, "Do you think you will be nervous?"

The Goose looked over at me and laughed. "Maybe on Friday." My son didn't want to ruin his Tuesday, Wednesday, and Thursday worrying about something that wasn't even going to happen until Friday. What a great lesson. I think I will keep him.

Your Right-Now Deal

Maybe your problem isn't looking in the rearview mirror; maybe your problem is looking in your crystal ball. But if you have one foot in the past and one foot in the future, you are *still* pooping all over the present. Tomorrow is not promised to us. Living mostly in the future will wreck your life.

Telling someone who is prone to overutilize crystal balls and rearview mirrors to simply "live in the moment" is like telling a homeless person to go buy a house. It's like telling a person who is yelling to simply calm down or like asking a parent to stop enabling his or her child. Living in the moment is an acquired taste and can require lots of practice. The good news is that, just like alcoholics can stop drinking, even the most dedicated viewer of crystal balls can learn to live in the present. While there are lots of tools to help with this, I want to suggest three that have been helpful to me and to some of my clients.

1. *Yoga.* If you would have told me a few years ago that I would ever be suggesting yoga in a book, I would have laughed. Back then, yoga seemed odd, Eastern, and for

young skinny girls, not an aging overweight man. Yet I will admit that what other people have been using for centuries works for me as well. While the theology of yoga doesn't work for me, the practice of yoga does. That is because my focus is on me and my mat at any given moment. I also love that it's physical in nature. When my body is engaged, it is easier to focus on my breathing and slow my thinking down. Yoga allows me to engage my body and focus my thinking in a way that most other activities do not.

2. *Mantras.* Many of my clients and friends have used short little statements to help them focus. Some refer to them as breath prayers, affirmations, or mantras. My friend Laney has said that she refocuses by repeatedly saying, "Right here…right now…I'm okay." Others mantras might be, "I am not alone," "It's okay," "Focus," "Breathe," or "God is near." The key is to find a mantra that works for or has meaning for you, and to repeat it to yourself when you are having trouble focusing on the present.

3. *Prayer and meditation.* Despite my history of faith, I've always struggled with prayer and meditation. Prayer and meditation work very well for lots of people. I have one friend who will pause when distracted and consider all of the sounds that he can hear in the moment—not in the past, but in the present moment. After forty-five seconds or so of that combined with several deep breaths, he opens his eyes and returns to work. He says the length of the exercise is determined by what it takes for him to begin to *feel* better. Taking a quiet moment to still one's mind and soul and pray or meditate can be a powerful way to ground one's self in the present.

When thinking about living in the present, it's important to understand that such living doesn't mean not having hopes, ambitions, goals, and dreams. In fact, these things are vital to living a full and healthy life. Rather, living in the present moment means recognizing that today is a right-now deal. Your life is a right-now deal. Life is not a dress rehearsal, and you do not have to be a slave to your crystal ball. All that any of us really has is this very moment. Don't waste it.

Questions to Consider

1. What do you think it means that our crystal balls are broken? Why do you think we are so bad at predicting the future?

2. What is your "crystal ball story"? When in your life have you had high expectations that were not met? What did that experience teach you?

3. How do you think focusing on our crystal balls prevents us from living today to the fullest?

4. Is there something that you know in your spirit you need to do right away? What's keeping you from doing it?

5. What hopes and dreams do you need to stop focusing so hard on, so you can live your life right now? How can you get one foot out of the future?

Chapter 7
The Swiss Army Knife of Health

What is your least favorite job or chore that you have to do on a regular basis? What job drives you crazy? For me, it has always been refilling the water softener salt. I *hate* refilling the water softener salt. For one thing, the small bags are about eight dollars each. Gold crystals might be worth that much, but salt? The bags are heavy. I'm old and fat and I take two bags at a time, which means I'm carrying eighty pounds of salt on my back. It hurts my shoulders, and then I have to take the bags down the basement stairs and not hit the drywall or take the bags down the back hill and not slip or step in dog poop. After that, I have to go back up and throw the empty bags in the trash. I hate everything about refilling the water softener salt.

But when I think about how much I hate refilling the water softener salt, I like to look at my left foot. Several years ago, the doctor was getting ready to cut it off. I had elective surgery on my left Achilles tendon. It was a routine surgery, but after a week or so, something was wrong. I didn't get better. In fact, I got worse. My foot looked horrible; it was red and swollen, and I was in excruciating pain. That Halloween ten days after surgery, I was lying on the front porch with my crutches handing out candy to kids, and I was in so much pain I could hardly even talk.

I went upstairs to bed, hoping the pain would subside. It was a struggle to get to sleep, and when I woke up at about three in the morning, I was in the most pain I've ever been in in my life. My blood pressure was 240 over 126 because of the pain. Now, I spent fifteen years working on an ambulance, so I'm smart enough to know that's not a good thing, and I'm married to a doctor who's smart enough to know that's not a good thing. That night I called the surgeon and said, "I think I'm in trouble. I'm getting ready to chew my own leg off."

He said, "Well, I need to see you, but I want you to come to Carmel." Carmel is not close to where I live, but I got in the car and drove up there. That drive was the hardest thing I'd done in a long time. I got there, and they gave me some medicine. My blood pressure went down, and the pain lessened. After three days, the staff sent me to surgery to have a "permanent" IV line inserted. I began a regimen of antibiotic treatments four times a day. While the doctors and I were both optimistic, more surgery lay ahead.

The infection had killed some of the tissue in my heel and was beginning to threaten the integrity of the tendon as well as the heel bone. There was some talk of my losing my foot, but short of that, another surgery would be scheduled to clean out the dead tissue. So after twenty days and countless IVs, pills, doctor appointments, dressing changes, and outbursts of frustration, I was headed back to surgery. After that surgery, what followed was about five weeks of receiving four IVs each day. I was sore, tired, and very slow to heal. I lived in bed just wishing that I could do things. I wasn't able to ride a bike, play racquetball, walk, or even work.

But in that moment, while I was lying in bed with an IV, I would have given anything to have hopped out of bed and refilled the water softener salt.

Finally, I was getting ready for another surgery on the same foot. Dr. Porter got down and prayed for my foot, and he looked at me and said, "I'm going to be honest with you. It takes healthy tissue to get the antibiotics in and it takes healthy tissue to get the infection out. Your problem is you don't have much healthy tissue. I'm going to do whatever I have to do, but I may have to take your foot."

I said, "Dave, don't do that. I need my foot."

The surgery center staff wheeled me back and gave me juice. Then, an hour or so later, I woke up and it was over. I was in the recovery room with no recollection. But I had one *really* important question at that point, as I looked down at the covers over my legs. I tried to wiggle my foot and could not. I tried to bump it and see if it hurt and could not feel a thing. Finally, I mashed the little red button to summon the nurse. She asked if I was okay, and I said I was really hot.

"Take those covers and pull them all the way off," I told the nurse. She pulled them off. I looked down and I saw my heavily wrapped foot. I said, "I'm good. Put them back." In time, I would once again get to refill the water softener salt.

"Have to" or "Get to"?

You see, the water softener salt is not something I *have* to do; it's something I *get* to do. If I had lost my foot, I would not have been able to do it. People always talk about what they have to do. Going to work is not something I have to do. It is something I get to do. Cleaning out a dying man's gutters is not something I have to do. It is something I get to do. Talking in a treatment center on a sunny day when I could be hiking is not something I have to do. It is something I get to do.

I once asked a man what he was doing over the weekend, and he said, "I have to go to a funeral."

I said, "Really? I'm sorry. Who died?"

"Rollie, a kid I grew up with. He was my best friend when we were little. He got mixed up in some bad stuff and he died. Now I've got to drive clear to that little town and spend all day Saturday at the funeral. I don't want to go, but I have to."

I looked at him and I said, "You do not *have* to do go to that funeral. You *get* to go to that funeral; that was your best friend. When you all were kids, you cut your thumbs and became blood brothers. You used to shoot squirrels together, play basketball together. You don't have to go to that funeral. You get to go to that funeral. It's going to be an honor to look his grieving mother in the eyes and give her a hug and say, 'I'm sorry.' You don't have to do that. You *get* to do that."

Recently a friend and mentor of mine was nearing the end of his life. The window for visiting him in the hospital was closing. His health and level of consciousness were both waning quickly. So I canceled a client and headed downtown to the VA Hospital to say my thanks and good-bye. When I walked in, he was mostly unconscious and he was hooked to oxygen, IVs, monitors, and other machines designed to prevent blood clots. I held his hand while I expressed my gratitude for the many hours together and lessons learned. There were tears of sorrow. Shortly after, I departed to the car with a hand full of tissues and a very heavy heart.

Nothing about that final visit was fun. I hate being sad. I hate crying. I hate saying good-bye. I always have. That visit cost me money because I canceled a client. Still, I wouldn't have missed it for the world. It would have been unthinkable for me to fumble the ball by passing on the opportunity to *get* to be with him one final time. I was grateful.

The Swiss Army Knife of Health: Gratitude

A Swiss army knife is considered a multipurpose tool. You can use it for just about anything; it's got all kinds of utensils on it. Well, there is a Swiss army knife that works on our moods too; in fact, it works for relationships, chronic pain, mood and thinking problems, and even trauma. The psychiatric Swiss army knife is *gratitude*.

A few years ago, I was sitting in the ER at Methodist Hospital with a guy who didn't know if he was on foot or on horseback. He was hearing voices and hallucinating; this guy didn't know if he was coming or going. I looked at this man and I said to him, "Tell me one thing that you're grateful for."

He said, "Well, my dog loves me. My dog's always there for me. My dog loves me and would never hurt me. I love my dog. My dog is very, very cool."

"So, what's your dog's name?"

"My dog would never hurt me; his name is Snoopy."

I wrote *dog, Snoopy* in big letters on a sheet of paper, and I said, "What else are you grateful for?"

He said, "I'm always able to eat; I'm on food stamps. They come every month, and that's very good. I'm able to eat because of food stamps."

I wrote, *Food stamps* on his paper sheet next to *dog, Snoopy*. Then I said, "I know you're scared. I know you're hearing voices. I know you're seeing things. That's okay. When you get super-duper scared, I just want you to look at these two things. I want you to be grateful for food stamps and your dog, Snoopy."

The man took a deep, soothing breath for the first time since I had entered the room and stared like a laser at what was written on his sheet.

Gratitude is a multipurpose tool for all of us. If you can't get grateful, then chances are that serenity, happiness, joy, and peace will all elude you. I know horrible things may have been done to you and you may have done some things that you didn't even think you were capable of. But you can still be grateful.

A lady called my office one time and she sobbed, "It's the worst day ever. My nineteen-year-old son got arrested. He just got married, and his wife got pregnant. She's going to leave him and take the baby. He's going to lose his job. It's just terrible; it's the worst thing ever."

I said, "How'd you sleep last night?"

She said, "It's kind of weird, but I slept well last night because it was the first time in six weeks that I knew where he was."

"So can you be grateful for a good night's sleep, grateful that you knew where your son was, that he isn't dead?" I said. "If that's the case, is it really the worst thing ever?"

There is always reason to be grateful, so find a way to be grateful. Make a gratitude list and keep it close. That's how I got over being chronically angry: It's hard to be pissed or afraid and grateful at the same time. On my phone in the little memo section, I have a gratitude list. There are about 300 things to be grateful for on my phone. When I'm full of fear, I can stop the world and go through the gratitude list, and if I really want to be spiritual, I try and pray through the gratitude list.

That list has become an amazing recovery tool. It allows me to develop some sense of peace and balance where once there was none, because I can't be grateful and mad at you at the same time. It's not going to happen. But here is the warning: Gratitude requires action. You have to write it down and you have to find a way to call time-out and reference that list in your life. What are two things that you're grateful for? Don't say family; family's got a name. Start thinking: What am I grateful for? Then write it down. Pray through the list. Pick up the phone and tell a friend the five things that you are grateful for right now. It's simple, but not easy. And it works.

Questions to Consider

1. Think about the things you always say you have to do. Do you really *have* to do them? Or do you *get* to do them?

2. How does realizing all of the things you *get* to do change your perspective on the routine tasks and responsibilities of life?

3. Why do you think gratitude is such a powerful tool in our lives? Why do you think it works in all areas of mental health?

4. Make a list of things you are grateful for, and use names. Keep that list with you so you can look at it when you are struggling or are full of fear.

Chapter 8
Focus on the Solution

One night shortly after my fortieth birthday, my wife and I were sitting in a nice restaurant preparing to order dinner. The lights were low, and the mood was right. I was hungry. But for the first time in my life, I was unable to read the menu. The words, printed in maroon ink on light blue paper, seemed to be out of focus. I didn't say anything about it that night, but the scenario kept happening. Each time, my frustration rose until at some point, I began to complain about not being able to read phone books, computer screens, documents at work, and a wide variety of other things. The worse it got, the more I would complain.

My poor vision eventually took its toll in other areas. I began to notice that my penmanship, which had never been very good, was deteriorating even further. I remember having a supervisor at the hospital ask if I had been in a hurry because my written assessment notes of a patient were hard to read. Another time I had taken some notes at a conference and was angry when I struggled to read them at home. My poor penmanship and bad vision was a challenging combination.

In time, it became clear that complaining more would not lead to better vision or handwriting. I eventually made an appointment with an eye doctor near my house who confirmed what I already knew: my vision wasn't very good anymore. The doctor explained that around age forty, most people experience deterioration in vision. There are no exercises or other things that can help. Laser surgery doesn't fix this type of problem. The problem was simple and so was the solution. It was time for me to be fitted for glasses. So for the past several years, I wear glasses whenever I want to see well.

Where Is Your Focus?

Many years ago, I heard a phrase that transformed how I viewed conflict and problems. The phrase was simple and direct: *Focus on the problem, and the problem gets bigger. Focus on the solution, and the solution gets bigger.*

At first, I thought the phrase was quaint and oversimplified, but at times when I was stuck or baffled, I began to look at where I was directing my attention. What I found was that all too often, I dedicated my time to lamenting, fueling, or obsessing over a problem. Doing this was taking up most of my time and nearly all of my energy. It was keeping me from ever getting to the solution. But then I realized that the choice about where to focus was simple, and that the decision about where to focus was all mine. I had the control.

For instance, I knew for several months before getting glasses that my vision was worsening, but instead of going to the eye doctor, I decided to complain, even though griping had no bearing on my sight. It is easier to complain about something than to fix it. As a counselor, I frequently begin sessions with new clients by asking, "What's a nice person like you doing with a guy like me on a day like this?" I'm able to break down their responses into one of several categories.

Some folks will instantly reach for the tissues and fight the tears that are welling up in their eyes. They have some level of shame, fear, or embarrassment about what has happened in the past, and often the process of working through it is both painful and scary. Other clients are more stoic and will matter-of-factly tell me the circumstances surrounding their wanting or needing to see a counselor. There is often a sense that they are emotionally detached from the identified issue. Some are well aware of what they believe the problem to be, yet they are unable to see their role in it. Clients often benefit from being able to tell their version of any situation without being interrupted. This seizes on the therapeutic factor known as *catharsis*. My favorite image of this is a disturbing one.

One week, my youngest son, The Midget, was traveling home from another state with some kids his age. They stopped for dinner at a cheap establishment and he ordered shrimp and scallops in pasta. As they made their way home, my son said he knew the food wasn't any good. "Dad, I just had to stick my finger down my throat and get rid of that nasty seafood. It was going to keep me sick," he reported. What he was really saying was that the

47

discomfort of throwing up was less than the discomfort of riding it out.

Life can be a lot like bad seafood. The only way to get relief from the feeling may be to go into the bathroom and stick your fingers down your throat. Therapy can be like that. Some clients feel better after just coming in and vomiting their story all at once.

Catharsis is one of Irvin Yalom's eleven therapeutic factors, but while catharsis alone can leave us feeling better, it is often not a long-term solution. It provides relief, but not healing. Often, after a person speaks his or her mind, little has changed. In fact, if nothing changes, a person will likely be upset again. One of the goals of therapy is to assist clients in shifting their focuses from the problem to the solution.

Not long ago, I had a couple in my office who was considering an intervention for their daughter. This young lady had experienced a romantic breakup in high school the same week that her grandmother died. That began a stint of periodic drinking and the use of marijuana. Her first year at college, the young lady slowly increased her use of substances. She was also sleeping around, especially after parties. One night she was sexually assaulted at a party, and her roommate noted that she had been either drunk or high ever since. "She just eats pills and drinks all the time," her friend reported.

Both parents were quite concerned that I would view their daughter as just a drug addict. The mom even went so far as to bring a photo album with their daughter's senior pictures in it. After looking at the pictures, the parents went on to detail how their daughter had managed to slide from being a good student in high school to failing classes in college. They noted a change in friends and activities. The mom cried as she mentioned a recent arrest and public embarrassment. After listening for a few minutes, I put my hand out like a traffic cop.

My suggestion was loving but firm: From that moment forward, we would spend nearly all of our time working to get their little girl into treatment and pointed toward a new and better life. We would no longer focus on the heartache, frustration, and pain that brought them to my office. What drove that family to my office was pain and fear. Pain is a great motivator. It is important not to save people from their pain, but pain is not the goal. Constructive pain causes a person to move toward a solution.

The 80/20 Rule

Are you familiar with the Pareto Principle? It comes from Italian economist Vilfredo Pareto who created a mathematical formula describing the unequal distribution of wealth in his country; he observed that 20 percent of the people owned 80 percent of the wealth. Since that time, the Pareto Principle (also known as the 80/20 rule) has been applied to a wide variety of subjects. The 80/20 rule can mean that in anything, a few things (20 percent) are vital, and many things (80 percent) are trivial. In America, Dr. Joseph Juran identified that 20 percent of manufacturing or scheduling errors caused 80 percent of problems. Project managers confirm that 20 percent of your work consumes 80 percent of your time and resources. You can apply the 80/20 rule to almost anything, from the science of management to the physical world.

This Pareto Principle can be useful in your life too. The 80/20 rule in therapy means that 80 percent of the time I spend talking with families is spent focusing on the solution. The other 20 percent I can talk about the past. Why is this so important? Let me explain: I hate math. I would have been happy if math never existed. Now, imagine that my son comes home from school one day, and I ask him about his math test. He gets his math ability from me.

He says, "Well, Dad, I think I flunked my math test."

And so the loving, kind, compassionate, well-adjusted person who I am looks at my son and yells, "How did you flunk your math test? Do you want to end up like your father? Math is important! You've got to do well at math! You're a Watson; it's not good enough to flunk your math test!"

This is just a story. My son is actually quite good at math. But would my yelling help him in math? I may feel better because of catharsis (though not really).

But what if, instead of yelling at him, I told him it was okay to miss the bus to stay after school and find a tutor? What if I told him to e-mail his teacher, or what if I asked my wife, who's

49

smarter than me, to help him with math? Wouldn't that be a better approach? If I do that, then I've put forth effort and service to the solution. A better life works the same way. If we just talk about all the crazy stuff we have done or the painful things that have been done to us, it can be entertaining or perhaps fun. It may even help us to tell our stories and get them off of our chests. We'll feel relief. But it won't make us better. We have to focus on the solution, focus on the 80 percent, because the 20 percent won't fix itself. If we focus on the problem, the problem will get bigger, but if we focus on the solution, the solution will get bigger. The choice is ours.

Questions to Consider

1. Think of a time when you had a choice to either focus on the problem or focus on the solution. Which did you do? What was the outcome?

2. How do you think pain—the 20 percent—can move a person toward a solution? How has pain motivated you to change a problem in your life?

3. Is it easy for you to devote only 20 percent of your focus to the problem, or is it hard to focus on the solution instead? Why?

4. Think of a problem you are facing in life right now. What would it look like for you to focus on the solution to that problem, rather than the problem itself?

Chapter 9
Ready, Set....

Alissa is one of my oldest friends. We met on a trip to Washington, DC, when we were high-school sophomores. Although we were from different towns, we became friends who kept in touch. Many years ago, she gave me a book of quotes. I still have that book somewhere, and—little did she know—many of those quotes would be significant to me over the years. One of the quotes from that book reads, "Success isn't final, and failure isn't fatal." That was new information to me, and it is still very hard for me to remember it.

I can have a slow patch at work and decide that I'm no good and that my work isn't worth it, when the truth is that business is only slow because the economy is challenging and nobody wants to spend Christmas in a treatment center. The same thing can happen when several of my clients relapse in a short period of time. I'm passionate about recovery and about the people whom I work with, so when clients struggle, I often wonder if I should have done something differently or if my work even mattered at all.

This was especially true one cold, late-winter day when my friend called to tell me about Kurt. Kurt was a guy I had known for a few years, and in recent weeks, I had agreed to work with him on a few issues, not as a client but as a friend. It was early in the morning, and my friend on the phone asked if I'd heard that Kurt was in the hospital. Innocently, I asked when he was going to be released. "He's not," my friend said. "He's probably going to die."

My heart sank. How could this be? Granted, my last communication with Kurt had illustrated the depth of his pain and struggle. But after thinking back over all of our calls, talks, and visits, there was no way I could have know that Kurt was going to take his own life.

The honor of speaking at Kurt's memorial service was more challenging that I could have imagined. Words which usually come easy for me seemed to be hiding in the shadows, like Kurt and his pain. Somehow, I got through it. As I was finishing, I looked at his young daughter who was seated in the front row clinging to every word I had to say about her father whom she had hardly known and who now was gone forever. As our eyes met, it was as if she saw my pain and love for her dad just as I saw hers. As I went back to my seat, I felt the strong urge to approach her. I knew enough not to ignore a feeling that strong. I walked toward her, still not sure why, but when I was three steps away, it came to me. I unfolded my speaking notes and placed them in her little hands, which were still wet from the tears that she was wiping away.

There are days when I still struggle with parts of this story. Today, my belief is that I made the very best of a very bad situation. I brought my best self. Sadly, each of us has days when our best self doesn't show up. We wish we could be our best selves, but we just aren't. There are seasons of life that, quite frankly, just stink.

Feeding hikers on the Appalachian Trail for the past thirteen summers, I have learned that there are an unending number of ways to walk from Georgia to Maine. The hikers have a saying: "Hike your own hike." Life is like that. Sometimes we have to take our own paths, but we are all still designed to live in some type of community. The previous chapters are not meant to tell you how to hike your hike or live your life. But even hikers who hike their own hike help each other; share information; and tell stories about what they have learned, what they fear, and what another might do to lessen the load or ease the burden. Some days on the trail are pretty; on some days, the views are amazing. Other days feature extreme temperatures, rain or snow, bugs, challenging wildlife, and poor sources of clean water. But even on the worst days, most hikers are given another chance to have a better tomorrow.

Many of the lessons in this book have given me another chance at life. I still make mistakes, often by allowing the worst of me to win out over the best that I might have to offer. But the lesson of the hikers can apply to us as well. Our job each day is to wake up, suit up, show up, and be the very best that we can be. You *get to* hike your own hike. Some days will feel easy; on some days, you will be amazing. Other days will be a challenge. But for every day, the words from Alissa's little book will apply: "Success isn't final, and failure isn't fatal."

Years ago, Alan Vickrey introduced me to a quote when I was a student in high school. It was a very tough time for me, and I felt like the school cared more about structure and reputation than students and results. In that place, Vic was an oasis of reality and perspective. Like my friend many years ago, Vic reminded me that I was human while challenging me to be and do my best. Vic used to say, "It's not important to do all things right as long as you do the right thing." All we've got is today. There's no use worrying about doing everything right. You are a hiker, and your path is set before you. So put down this book. *Gratefully* go and hike the journey set before you. And remember: You don't have to do it alone.

Questions to Consider

1. Consider the quote, "Success isn't final, and failure isn't fatal." How do you think believing or not believing this quote affects the way people live their lives?

2. Sometimes, when faced with failure, it's easy to believe that the work you do does not matter. Do you buy into this lie? What can you do to help free yourself from it?

3. In the end, we all have to "hike our own hike." What about your hike do you think makes it different from anyone else's hike?

4. What are three lessons you have learned from this book? How can you begin to apply these lessons in your life this week?

Acknowledgements

No book just happens. This one is no different.

I'm grateful to God for laying out the journey and being there to always redeem the missed turns along the way. I'm grateful for my wife, Maureen, who has stayed with me during many long seasons when I didn't deserve her love or commitment. Where has the time gone? Thanks for your encouragement and support.

To The Goose and The Midget, who have provided love, challenges, laughs, tastes and textures, flavors, and meaning to my life. Being your dad has been the greatest honor of my life. I so wish I could have done a better job. I hope you both know the wonderful things that you are capable of doing!

To Stephanie Hill, who took my talks and made sense of them. Your patience and talent remain a huge blessing. Thanks. Your journey will include many other books, and those who enjoy them will be better for the experience. Thanks for all of your help and willingness.

To Marion O. R., who has informed my journey with his life, example, and writings. You have made me a better therapist. *Thank you* seems both insufficient and unnecessary because of the God you serve. Your work will outlive you, and this book clearly reflects your work in many ways.

To Mike D., who has been a friend and mentor. I'm a better therapist because of your willingness to share both personally and professionally. Someday I hope to impact another as you have impacted me.

To others who have shaped my journey, there are simply not enough words. There are too many of you to mention you all: David R., Mark S., a different Mark S., Scott I., "Del" and his family, Dick, Vic, Eddie, Rip, KLB, DAA, David S., Jerry A., Slug, Dean J., Mike G., Paul G., Dean K., Mike G., Steve K., the racquetball guys, Monday small group, camp friends, and the many whom I've met serving meals on the ATM.

I continue to enjoy a great God, family, friends, and the journey. As a result, more shall be revealed.

About the Authors

Scott J. Watson is a Licensed Clinical Addictions Counselor and founder of Heartland Intervention, LLC, in Indianapolis, IN. In addition to his private practice, Scott has previously worked as an Employee Assistance Professional and has been an Assessment Specialist in a busy urban trauma center.

Known for taking a caring but firm approach with clients, Scott is a frequent trainer and speaker. He is also a regular contributor to several radio and television stations throughout Central Indiana. In 1999, he published *The Court Report: Stories from the bleachers, fields, and penalty boxes of life*. In 2014, he coauthored *I Need Help: Solutions to combat youth suicide in Indiana* with Sen. Jim Merritt.

Scott lives in Indianapolis with his family. He enjoys hillbilly music, gardening, racquetball, hiking, and cooking. Learn more at www.heartlandintervention.com.

Stephanie Hill is a freelance writer and editor in the Chicago area. She has played a part in editing several nonfiction books, in association with Tyndale House Publishers and on her own.

On top of her nonfiction editing work, Stephanie has written three fiction novels and is a leader and participant in local writing and literacy iniatives, such as National Novel Writing Month and the Young Writers' Literary Journal.

Stephanie lives in the Chicago area, where she enjoys writing, reading, and a proliferation of coffee houses.

Made in the USA
Columbia, SC
09 June 2023

17786135R00033